T5-CCU-032

What's Underneath?

Contents

Under Your Feet 2

Under a House 4

Under a Garden 6

Under a Street 8

Under a City 10

Under the Sea 12

Under the Seabed 14

Index 16

Rigby

Under Your Feet

burrow

tunnel

There is another world under the ground.
Under your feet, there may be animals living
in burrows, or people working in tunnels.

Under a House

electricity cable

gas pipe

water pipe

sewage

Under a house, there are cables and pipes.
The cables carry electricity for lights and TVs.
Gas pipes carry gas to stoves. Water pipes
carry water to bathrooms and sinks.

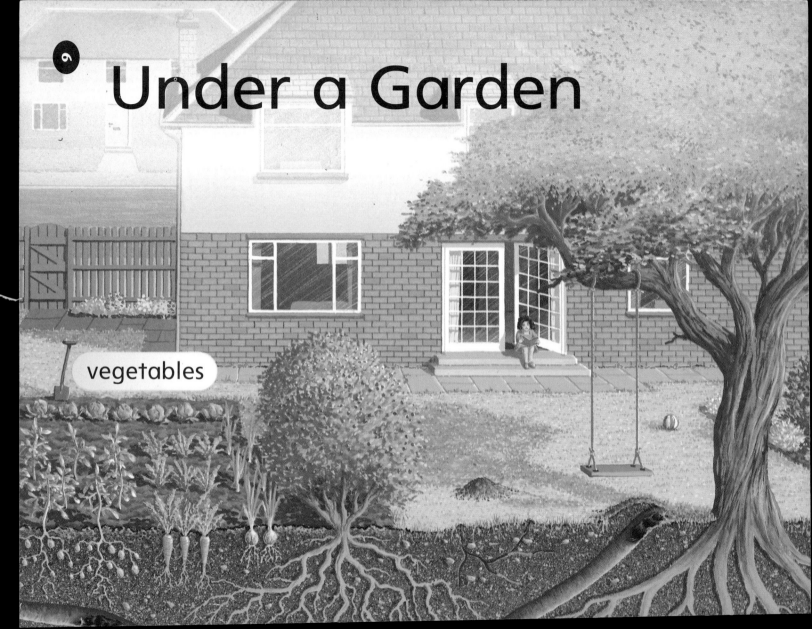

Under a Garden

vegetables

roots

Under a garden, roots of plants and trees spread through the soil. Some vegetables, like potatoes and carrots, grow under the ground. Sometimes a mole digs up the lawn.

Under a Street

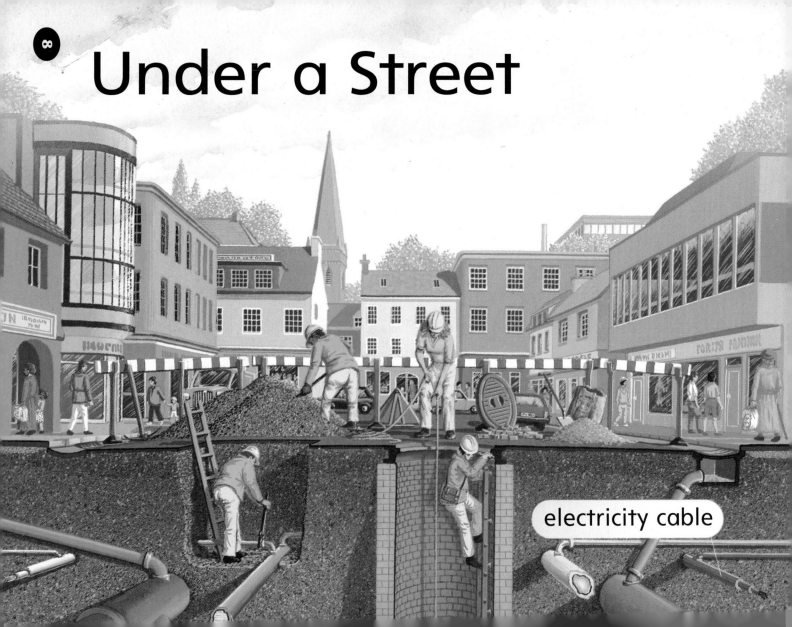

electricity cable

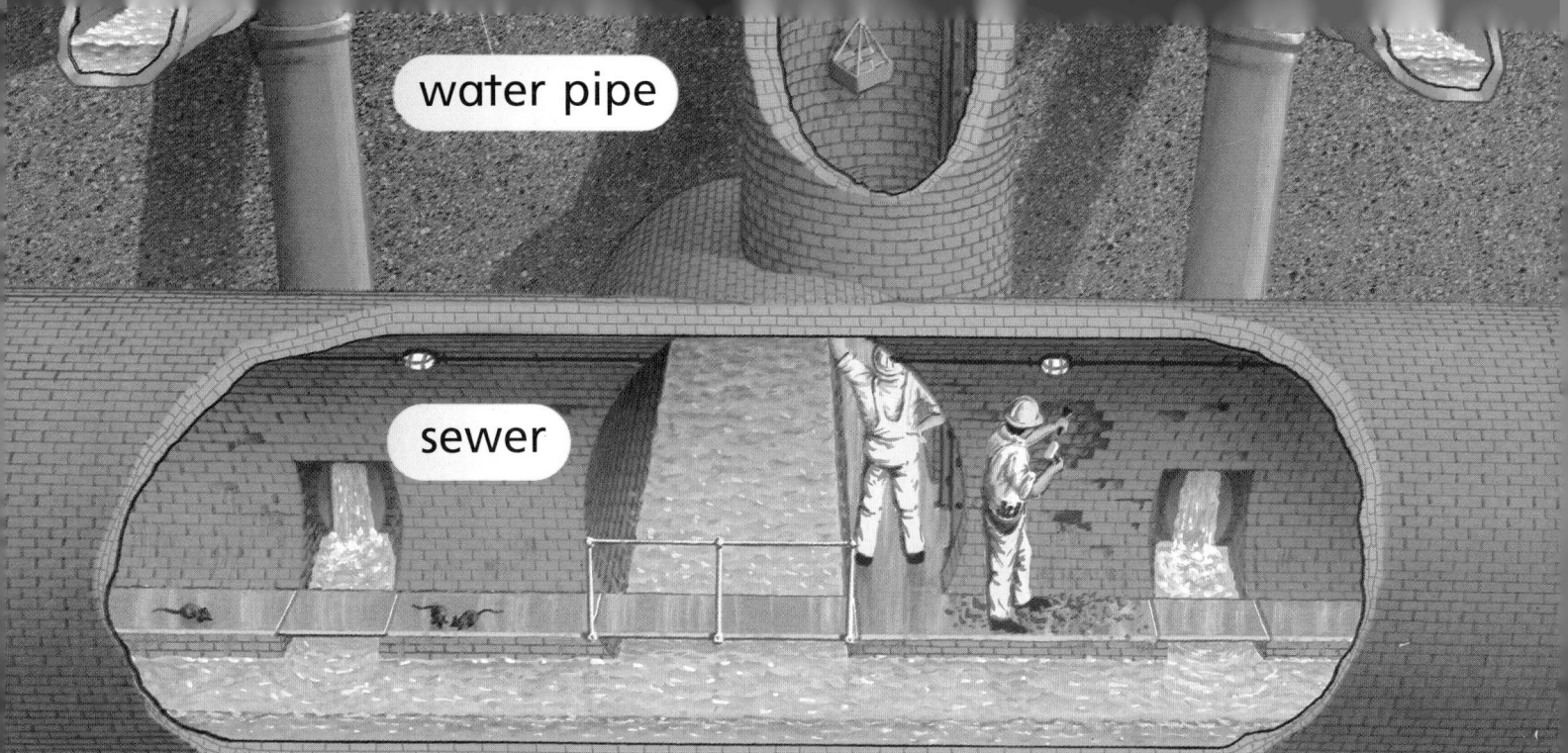

water pipe

sewer

Under a street, there are pipes called sewers. Sewers take away the dirty water and waste from factories, houses, and streets. Workers climb down through holes into the sewers.

Under a City

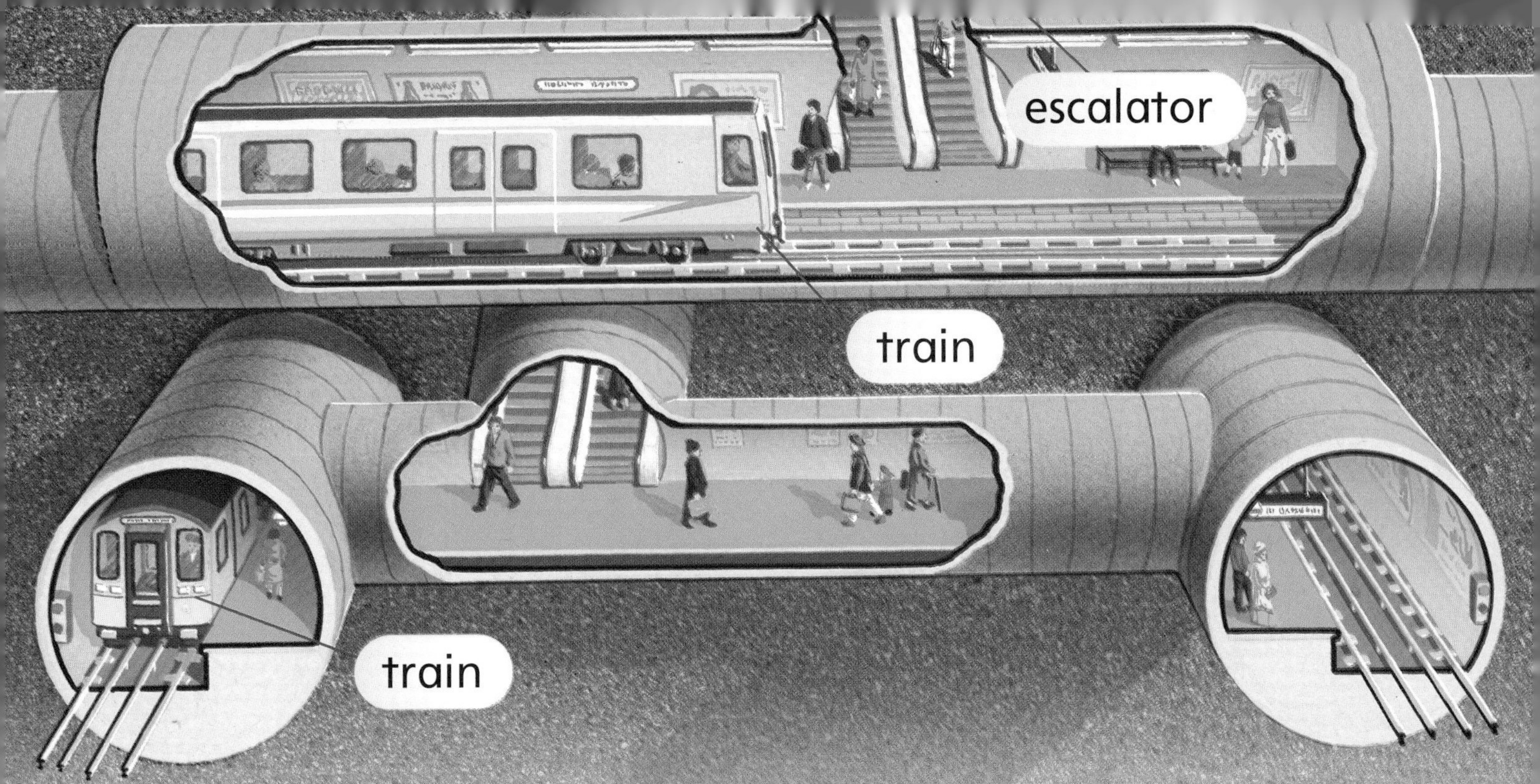

escalator

train

train

Under this city, there are train stations with platforms. Moving stairs called escalators take people up and down between the street and the trains.

Under the Sea

net

submarine

shipwreck

Under the sea, plants grow and fish swim.
Nets hang down from boats to catch fish.
Sometimes divers and submarines explore
shipwrecks.

Under the Seabed

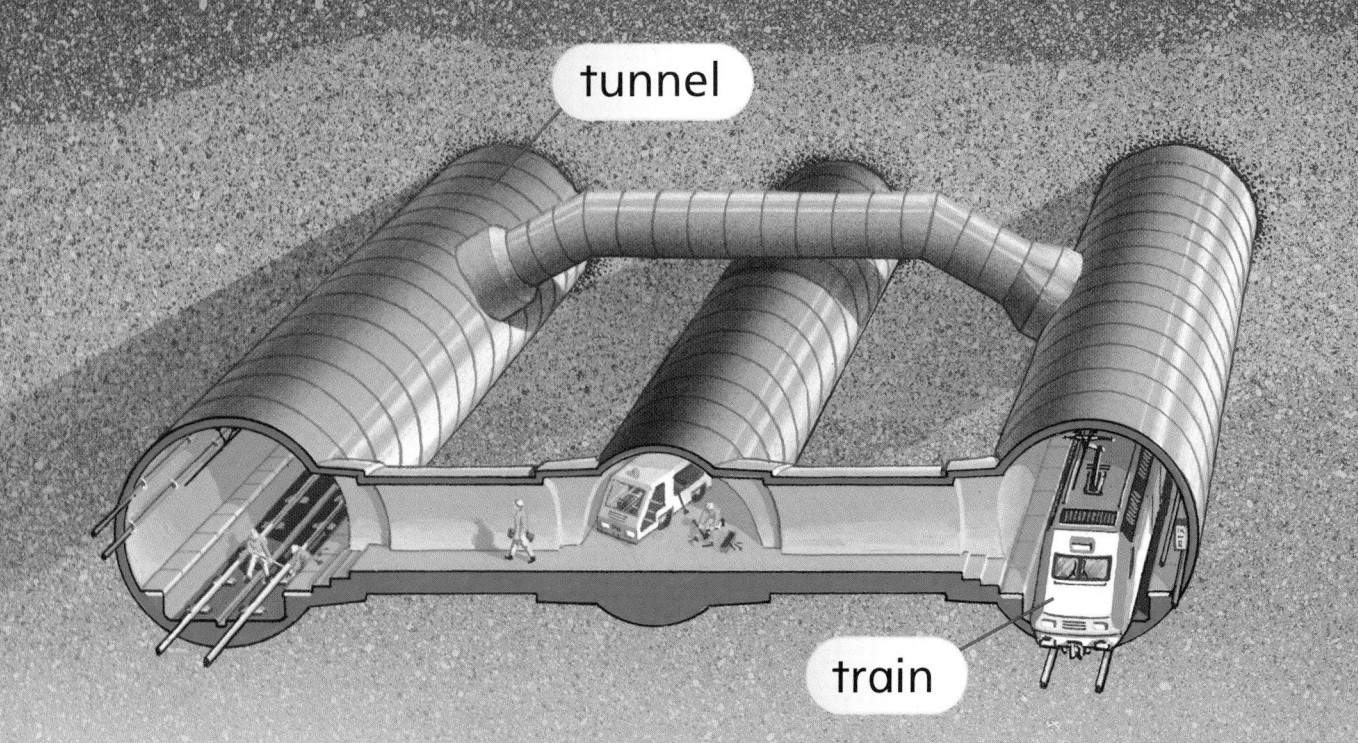

tunnel

train

Under the seabed, tunnels run from England
to France. Trains go through the tunnels.
They carry people, cars, and trucks.

15

Index

a
b
c
d
e
f
g
h
i
j
k
l
m
n
o
p
q
r
s
t
u
v
w
x
y
z

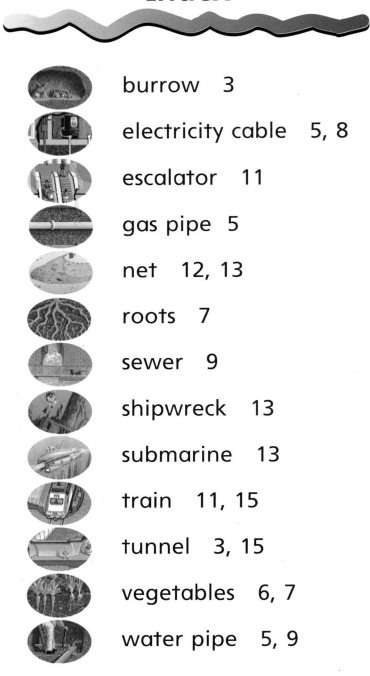

burrow   3

electricity cable   5, 8

escalator   11

gas pipe   5

net   12, 13

roots   7

sewer   9

shipwreck   13

submarine   13

train   11, 15

tunnel   3, 15

vegetables   6, 7

water pipe   5, 9